NOTARY PUBLIC JOURNAL

NOTARY LOG

Date	Signer's Name (Print)	Document Type (Lease /Warrant)	Type of ID Produced & Number (drivers license #)	ID Expiration Date

NOTARY LOG

Date	Signer's Name (Print)	Document Type (Lease /Warrant)	Type of ID Produced & Number (drivers license #)	ID Expiration Date

NOTARY LOG

Date	Signer's Name (Print)	Document Type (Lease /Warrant)	Type of ID Produced & Number (drivers license #)	ID Expiration Date

NOTARY LOG

Date	Signer's Name (Print)	Document Type (Lease /Warrant)	Type of ID Produced & Number (drivers license #)	ID Expiration Date

NOTARY LOG

Date	Signer's Name (Print)	Document Type (Lease /Warrant)	Type of ID Produced & Number (drivers license #)	ID Expiration Date

NOTARY LOG

Date	Signer's Name (Print)	Document Type (Lease /Warrant)	Type of ID Produced & Number (drivers license #)	ID Expiration Date

NOTARY LOG

Date	Signer's Name (Print)	Document Type (Lease /Warrant)	Type of ID Produced & Number (drivers license #)	ID Expiration Date

NOTARY LOG

Date	Signer's Name (Print)	Document Type (Lease /Warrant)	Type of ID Produced & Number (drivers license #)	ID Expiration Date

NOTARY LOG

Date	Signer's Name (Print)	Document Type (Lease /Warrant)	Type of ID Produced & Number (drivers license #)	ID Expiration Date

NOTARY LOG

Date	Signer's Name (Print)	Document Type (Lease /Warrant)	Type of ID Produced & Number (drivers license #)	ID Expiration Date

NOTARY LOG

Date	Signer's Name (Print)	Document Type (Lease /Warrant)	Type of ID Produced & Number (drivers license #)	ID Expiration Date

NOTARY LOG

Date	Signer's Name (Print)	Document Type (Lease /Warrant)	Type of ID Produced & Number (drivers license #)	ID Expiration Date

NOTARY LOG

Date	Signer's Name (Print)	Document Type (Lease /Warrant)	Type of ID Produced & Number (drivers license #)	ID Expiration Date

NOTARY LOG

Date	Signer's Name (Print)	Document Type (Lease /Warrant)	Type of ID Produced & Number (drivers license #)	ID Expiration Date

NOTARY LOG

Date	Signer's Name (Print)	Document Type (Lease /Warrant)	Type of ID Produced & Number (drivers license #)	ID Expiration Date

NOTARY LOG

Date	Signer's Name (Print)	Document Type (Lease /Warrant)	Type of ID Produced & Number (drivers license #)	ID Expiration Date

NOTARY LOG

Date	Signer's Name (Print)	Document Type (Lease /Warrant)	Type of ID Produced & Number (drivers license #)	ID Expiration Date

NOTARY LOG

Date	Signer's Name (Print)	Document Type (Lease /Warrant)	Type of ID Produced & Number (drivers license #)	ID Expiration Date

NOTARY LOG

Date	Signer's Name (Print)	Document Type (Lease /Warrant)	Type of ID Produced & Number (drivers license #)	ID Expiration Date

NOTARY LOG

Date	Signer's Name (Print)	Document Type (Lease /Warrant)	Type of ID Produced & Number (drivers license #)	ID Expiration Date

NOTARY LOG

Date	Signer's Name (Print)	Document Type (Lease /Warrant)	Type of ID Produced & Number (drivers license #)	ID Expiration Date

NOTARY LOG

Date	Signer's Name (Print)	Document Type (Lease /Warrant)	Type of ID Produced & Number (drivers license #)	ID Expiration Date

NOTARY LOG

Date	Signer's Name (Print)	Document Type (Lease /Warrant)	Type of ID Produced & Number (drivers license #)	ID Expiration Date

NOTARY LOG

Date	Signer's Name (Print)	Document Type (Lease /Warrant)	Type of ID Produced & Number (drivers license #)	ID Expiration Date

NOTARY LOG

Date	Signer's Name (Print)	Document Type (Lease /Warrant)	Type of ID Produced & Number (drivers license #)	ID Expiration Date

NOTARY LOG

Date	Signer's Name (Print)	Document Type (Lease /Warrant)	Type of ID Produced & Number (drivers license #)	ID Expiration Date

NOTARY LOG

Date	Signer's Name (Print)	Document Type (Lease /Warrant)	Type of ID Produced & Number (drivers license #)	ID Expiration Date

NOTARY LOG

Date	Signer's Name (Print)	Document Type (Lease /Warrant)	Type of ID Produced & Number (drivers license #)	ID Expiration Date

NOTARY LOG

Date	Signer's Name (Print)	Document Type (Lease /Warrant)	Type of ID Produced & Number (drivers license #)	ID Expiration Date

NOTARY LOG

Date	Signer's Name (Print)	Document Type (Lease /Warrant)	Type of ID Produced & Number (drivers license #)	ID Expiration Date

NOTARY LOG

Date	Signer's Name (Print)	Document Type (Lease /Warrant)	Type of ID Produced & Number (drivers license #)	ID Expiration Date

NOTARY LOG

Date	Signer's Name (Print)	Document Type (Lease /Warrant)	Type of ID Produced & Number (drivers license #)	ID Expiration Date

NOTARY LOG

Date	Signer's Name (Print)	Document Type (Lease /Warrant)	Type of ID Produced & Number (drivers license #)	ID Expiration Date

NOTARY LOG

Date	Signer's Name (Print)	Document Type (Lease /Warrant)	Type of ID Produced & Number (drivers license #)	ID Expiration Date

NOTARY LOG

Date	Signer's Name (Print)	Document Type (Lease /Warrant)	Type of ID Produced & Number (drivers license #)	ID Expiration Date

NOTARY LOG

Date	Signer's Name (Print)	Document Type (Lease /Warrant)	Type of ID Produced & Number (drivers license #)	ID Expiration Date

NOTARY LOG

Date	Signer's Name (Print)	Document Type (Lease /Warrant)	Type of ID Produced & Number (drivers license #)	ID Expiration Date

NOTARY LOG

Date	Signer's Name (Print)	Document Type (Lease /Warrant)	Type of ID Produced & Number (drivers license #)	ID Expiration Date

NOTARY LOG

Date	Signer's Name (Print)	Document Type (Lease /Warrant)	Type of ID Produced & Number (drivers license #)	ID Expiration Date

NOTARY LOG

Date	Signer's Name (Print)	Document Type (Lease /Warrant)	Type of ID Produced & Number (drivers license #)	ID Expiration Date

NOTARY LOG

Date	Signer's Name (Print)	Document Type (Lease /Warrant)	Type of ID Produced & Number (drivers license #)	ID Expiration Date

NOTARY LOG

Date	Signer's Name (Print)	Document Type (Lease /Warrant)	Type of ID Produced & Number (drivers license #)	ID Expiration Date

NOTARY LOG

Date	Signer's Name (Print)	Document Type (Lease /Warrant)	Type of ID Produced & Number (drivers license #)	ID Expiration Date

NOTARY LOG

Date	Signer's Name (Print)	Document Type (Lease /Warrant)	Type of ID Produced & Number (drivers license #)	ID Expiration Date

NOTARY LOG

Date	Signer's Name (Print)	Document Type (Lease /Warrant)	Type of ID Produced & Number (drivers license #)	ID Expiration Date

NOTARY LOG

Date	Signer's Name (Print)	Document Type (Lease /Warrant)	Type of ID Produced & Number (drivers license #)	ID Expiration Date

NOTARY LOG

Date	Signer's Name (Print)	Document Type (Lease /Warrant)	Type of ID Produced & Number (drivers license #)	ID Expiration Date

NOTARY LOG

Date	Signer's Name (Print)	Document Type (Lease /Warrant)	Type of ID Produced & Number (drivers license #)	ID Expiration Date

NOTARY LOG

Date	Signer's Name (Print)	Document Type (Lease /Warrant)	Type of ID Produced & Number (drivers license #)	ID Expiration Date

NOTARY LOG

Date	Signer's Name (Print)	Document Type (Lease /Warrant)	Type of ID Produced & Number (drivers license #)	ID Expiration Date

NOTARY LOG

Date	Signer's Name (Print)	Document Type (Lease /Warrant)	Type of ID Produced & Number (drivers license #)	ID Expiration Date

NOTARY LOG

Date	Signer's Name (Print)	Document Type (Lease /Warrant)	Type of ID Produced & Number (drivers license #)	ID Expiration Date

NOTARY LOG

Date	Signer's Name (Print)	Document Type (Lease /Warrant)	Type of ID Produced & Number (drivers license #)	ID Expiration Date

NOTARY LOG

Date	Signer's Name (Print)	Document Type (Lease /Warrant)	Type of ID Produced & Number (drivers license #)	ID Expiration Date

NOTARY LOG

Date	Signer's Name (Print)	Document Type (Lease /Warrant)	Type of ID Produced & Number (drivers license #)	ID Expiration Date

NOTARY LOG

Date	Signer's Name (Print)	Document Type (Lease /Warrant)	Type of ID Produced & Number (drivers license #)	ID Expiration Date

NOTARY LOG

Date	Signer's Name (Print)	Document Type (Lease /Warrant)	Type of ID Produced & Number (drivers license #)	ID Expiration Date

NOTARY LOG

Date	Signer's Name (Print)	Document Type (Lease /Warrant)	Type of ID Produced & Number (drivers license #)	ID Expiration Date

NOTARY LOG

Date	Signer's Name (Print)	Document Type (Lease /Warrant)	Type of ID Produced & Number (drivers license #)	ID Expiration Date

NOTARY LOG

Date	Signer's Name (Print)	Document Type (Lease /Warrant)	Type of ID Produced & Number (drivers license #)	ID Expiration Date

NOTARY LOG

Date	Signer's Name (Print)	Document Type (Lease /Warrant)	Type of ID Produced & Number (drivers license #)	ID Expiration Date

NOTARY LOG

Date	Signer's Name (Print)	Document Type (Lease /Warrant)	Type of ID Produced & Number (drivers license #)	ID Expiration Date

NOTARY LOG

Date	Signer's Name (Print)	Document Type (Lease /Warrant)	Type of ID Produced & Number (drivers license #)	ID Expiration Date

NOTARY LOG

Date	Signer's Name (Print)	Document Type (Lease /Warrant)	Type of ID Produced & Number (drivers license #)	ID Expiration Date

NOTARY LOG

Date	Signer's Name (Print)	Document Type (Lease /Warrant)	Type of ID Produced & Number (drivers license #)	ID Expiration Date

NOTARY LOG

Date	Signer's Name (Print)	Document Type (Lease /Warrant)	Type of ID Produced & Number (drivers license #)	ID Expiration Date

NOTARY LOG

Date	Signer's Name (Print)	Document Type (Lease /Warrant)	Type of ID Produced & Number (drivers license #)	ID Expiration Date

NOTARY LOG

Date	Signer's Name (Print)	Document Type (Lease /Warrant)	Type of ID Produced & Number (drivers license #)	ID Expiration Date

NOTARY LOG

Date	Signer's Name (Print)	Document Type (Lease /Warrant)	Type of ID Produced & Number (drivers license #)	ID Expiration Date

NOTARY LOG

Date	Signer's Name (Print)	Document Type (Lease /Warrant)	Type of ID Produced & Number (drivers license #)	ID Expiration Date

NOTARY LOG

Date	Signer's Name (Print)	Document Type (Lease /Warrant)	Type of ID Produced & Number (drivers license #)	ID Expiration Date

NOTARY LOG

Date	Signer's Name (Print)	Document Type (Lease /Warrant)	Type of ID Produced & Number (drivers license #)	ID Expiration Date

NOTARY LOG

Date	Signer's Name (Print)	Document Type (Lease /Warrant)	Type of ID Produced & Number (drivers license #)	ID Expiration Date

NOTARY LOG

Date	Signer's Name (Print)	Document Type (Lease /Warrant)	Type of ID Produced & Number (drivers license #)	ID Expiration Date

NOTARY LOG

Date	Signer's Name (Print)	Document Type (Lease /Warrant)	Type of ID Produced & Number (drivers license #)	ID Expiration Date

NOTARY LOG

Date	Signer's Name (Print)	Document Type (Lease /Warrant)	Type of ID Produced & Number (drivers license #)	ID Expiration Date

NOTARY LOG

Date	Signer's Name (Print)	Document Type (Lease /Warrant)	Type of ID Produced & Number (drivers license #)	ID Expiration Date

NOTARY LOG

Date	Signer's Name (Print)	Document Type (Lease /Warrant)	Type of ID Produced & Number (drivers license #)	ID Expiration Date

NOTARY LOG

Date	Signer's Name (Print)	Document Type (Lease /Warrant)	Type of ID Produced & Number (drivers license #)	ID Expiration Date

NOTARY LOG

Date	Signer's Name (Print)	Document Type (Lease /Warrant)	Type of ID Produced & Number (drivers license #)	ID Expiration Date

NOTARY LOG

Date	Signer's Name (Print)	Document Type (Lease /Warrant)	Type of ID Produced & Number (drivers license #)	ID Expiration Date

NOTARY LOG

Date	Signer's Name (Print)	Document Type (Lease /Warrant)	Type of ID Produced & Number (drivers license #)	ID Expiration Date

NOTARY LOG

Date	Signer's Name (Print)	Document Type (Lease /Warrant)	Type of ID Produced & Number (drivers license #)	ID Expiration Date

NOTARY LOG

Date	Signer's Name (Print)	Document Type (Lease /Warrant)	Type of ID Produced & Number (drivers license #)	ID Expiration Date

NOTARY LOG

Date	Signer's Name (Print)	Document Type (Lease /Warrant)	Type of ID Produced & Number (drivers license #)	ID Expiration Date

NOTARY LOG

Date	Signer's Name (Print)	Document Type (Lease /Warrant)	Type of ID Produced & Number (drivers license #)	ID Expiration Date

NOTARY LOG

Date	Signer's Name (Print)	Document Type (Lease /Warrant)	Type of ID Produced & Number (drivers license #)	ID Expiration Date

NOTARY LOG

Date	Signer's Name (Print)	Document Type (Lease /Warrant)	Type of ID Produced & Number (drivers license #)	ID Expiration Date

NOTARY LOG

Date	Signer's Name (Print)	Document Type (Lease /Warrant)	Type of ID Produced & Number (drivers license #)	ID Expiration Date

NOTARY LOG

Date	Signer's Name (Print)	Document Type (Lease /Warrant)	Type of ID Produced & Number (drivers license #)	ID Expiration Date

NOTARY LOG

Date	Signer's Name (Print)	Document Type (Lease /Warrant)	Type of ID Produced & Number (drivers license #)	ID Expiration Date

NOTARY LOG

Date	Signer's Name (Print)	Document Type (Lease /Warrant)	Type of ID Produced & Number (drivers license #)	ID Expiration Date

NOTARY LOG

Date	Signer's Name (Print)	Document Type (Lease /Warrant)	Type of ID Produced & Number (drivers license #)	ID Expiration Date

NOTARY LOG

Date	Signer's Name (Print)	Document Type (Lease /Warrant)	Type of ID Produced & Number (drivers license #)	ID Expiration Date

NOTARY LOG

Date	Signer's Name (Print)	Document Type (Lease /Warrant)	Type of ID Produced & Number (drivers license #)	ID Expiration Date

NOTARY LOG

Date	Signer's Name (Print)	Document Type (Lease /Warrant)	Type of ID Produced & Number (drivers license #)	ID Expiration Date

NOTARY LOG

Date	Signer's Name (Print)	Document Type (Lease /Warrant)	Type of ID Produced & Number (drivers license #)	ID Expiration Date

NOTARY LOG

Date	Signer's Name (Print)	Document Type (Lease /Warrant)	Type of ID Produced & Number (drivers license #)	ID Expiration Date

NOTARY LOG

Date	Signer's Name (Print)	Document Type (Lease /Warrant)	Type of ID Produced & Number (drivers license #)	ID Expiration Date

NOTARY LOG

Date	Signer's Name (Print)	Document Type (Lease /Warrant)	Type of ID Produced & Number (drivers license #)	ID Expiration Date

NOTARY LOG

Date	Signer's Name (Print)	Document Type (Lease /Warrant)	Type of ID Produced & Number (drivers license #)	ID Expiration Date

NOTARY LOG

Date	Signer's Name (Print)	Document Type (Lease /Warrant)	Type of ID Produced & Number (drivers license #)	ID Expiration Date

NOTARY LOG

Date	Signer's Name (Print)	Document Type (Lease /Warrant)	Type of ID Produced & Number (drivers license #)	ID Expiration Date

NOTARY LOG

Date	Signer's Name (Print)	Document Type (Lease /Warrant)	Type of ID Produced & Number (drivers license #)	ID Expiration Date

www.ingramcontent.com/pod-product-compliance
Lightning Source LLC
LaVergne TN
LVHW060823170826
845678LV00010B/1888
* 9 7 9 8 8 6 9 4 5 5 3 3 8 *